AXIS PARENT GUIDES SERIES

PARENT GUIDE BUNDLES

A PARENT'S GUIDE TO
RACISM IN THE UNITED STATES

A PARENT'S GUIDE TO

RACISM IN THE UNITED STATES

Tyndale House Publishers
Carol Stream, Illinois

Visit Tyndale online at tyndale.com.

Visit Axis online at axis.org.

Tyndale and Tyndale's quill logo are registered trademarks of Tyndale House Ministries.

A Parent's Guide to Racism in the United States

Designed by Lindsey Bergsma

Scripture quotations are from The ESV® Bible (The Holy Bible, English Standard Version®), copyright © 2001 by Crossway, a publishing ministry of Good News Publishers. Used by permission. All rights reserved.

For information about special discounts for bulk purchases, please contact Tyndale House Publishers at csresponse@tyndale.com, or call 1-855-277-9400.

Library of Congress Cataloging-in-Publication Data

A catalog record for this book is available from the Library of Congress.

ISBN 978-1-4964-6782-9

Printed in the United States of America

29	28	27	26	25	24	23
7	6	5	4	3	2	1

How curious a land is this,—how full of untold story, of tragedy and laughter, and the rich legacy of human life; shadowed with a tragic past, and big with future promise!

THE SOULS OF BLACK FOLK
BY W. E. B. DU BOIS

CONTENTS

A LETTER FROM AXIS

Dear Reader,

We're Axis, and since 2007, we've been creating resources to help connect parents, teens, and Jesus in a disconnected world. We're a group of gospel-minded researchers, speakers, and content creators, and we're excited to bring you the best of what we've learned about making meaningful connections with the teens in your life.

This parent's guide is designed to help start a conversation. Our goal is to give you enough knowledge that you're able to ask your teen informed questions about their world. For each guide, we spend weeks reading, researching, and interviewing parents and teens in order to distill everything you need to know about the topic at hand. We encourage you to read the whole thing and then to use the questions we include to get the conversation going with your teen—and then to follow the conversation wherever it leads.

As Douglas Stone, Bruce Patton, and Sheila Heen point out in their book *Difficult Conversations*, "Changes in attitudes and behavior rarely come about because of arguments, facts, and attempts to persuade. How often do *you* change your values and beliefs—or whom you love or what you want in life—based on something someone tells you? And how likely are you to do so when the person who is trying to change you doesn't seem fully aware of the reasons you see things differently in the first place?"[1] For whatever reason, when we believe that others are trying to understand *our* point of view, our defenses usually go down, and we're more willing to listen to *their* point of view. The rising generation is no exception.

So we encourage you to ask questions, to listen, and then to share your heart with your teen. As we often say at Axis, discipleship happens where conversation happens.

Sincerely,
Your friends at Axis

---

[1] Douglas Stone, Bruce Patton, and Sheila Heen, *Difficult Conversations: How to Discuss What Matters Most*, rev. ed. (New York: Penguin Books, 2010), 137.

NATIONS, KINDREDS, PEOPLE, TONGUES

IN APRIL OF 2019, the Pew Research Center released a report called "Race in America," which gave an overview of how Americans thought about racial issues in our nation. According to the survey, 58 percent of people say that race relations are going poorly. Fifty-six percent say that being Black hurts a person's chances of getting ahead in life, and 51 percent agree with the same statement regarding Hispanic people. Sixty-five percent of Americans agree that it's more common to hear people expressing racist views or sentiments than it used to be. Seventy-six percent of Black people, 76 percent of Asian people, and 58 percent of Hispanic people say they experience race-based discrimination "at least from time to time."[1]

Add to that the deaths of George Floyd and Breonna Taylor in 2020, the increase in violent crimes against Asian Americans in the wake of the COVID-19 pandemic, and the unethical treatment of immigrants at the border, and it's no wonder this has become such a massive conversation.

The purpose of this guide is not to give a definitive solution to the problem of racism, to give a history of racism, or to unpack every way racism may intertwine with our social systems today. At Axis, our goal is always to equip parents and caring adults with information and confidence to have conversations with the teens in their lives. We want you to be ready when the topic of racism arises, so this guide is based on a biblical understanding of what racism is and how we as Christians are called to respond to it. Our goal is for you to be able to create a

We want you to be ready when the topic of racism arises, so this guide is based on a biblical understanding of what racism is and how we as Christians are called to respond to it.

space where you can talk about the difficult topic of race in a way that creates empathy and understanding in both your teen and yourself—and ultimately brings glory to God.

WHAT IS RACISM?

RACISM IS DISCRIMINATION against a person or group of people based solely on their race or ethnicity. Most often, racism is perpetrated by a person or group with more status, influence, wealth, power, or leverage than another person or group. Racism can be on an individual level, when one person thinks or behaves in harmful ways toward others of a different race, or it can exist on a higher level, when racial discrimination motivates lawmaking or judicial rulings that remain in effect over time.

Slavery of African people is what many think of when the topic of racism is brought up, but racism has affected many aspects of our nation's history. Native Americans were subjected to atrocities like the Trail of Tears, Japanese Americans who had lived in their homes for generations were forced into internment camps during World War II, and the terrorist attacks of 9/11 incited a huge wave of anti-Arab sentiment that led to a 500 percent spike in hate crimes against anyone suspected of being Muslim.[2]

Racism has divided America perhaps more than any other issue. This is at least in part due to the fact that racism has been present in many of the structures that underpin our country. Although Black men's right to vote was passed into law in 1870, state laws and practices made this almost impossible for many years. In some places, Black people were forced to recite the entire Constitution before they were allowed to vote or simply told that they'd showed up to the wrong polling place or come at the wrong time, even though these things weren't true.[3] The Voting Rights Act, which prohibited these practices, wasn't signed into law until

No one wants to be called a racist, and no one wants to believe it about themselves. But refusing to discuss a problem never makes it go away.

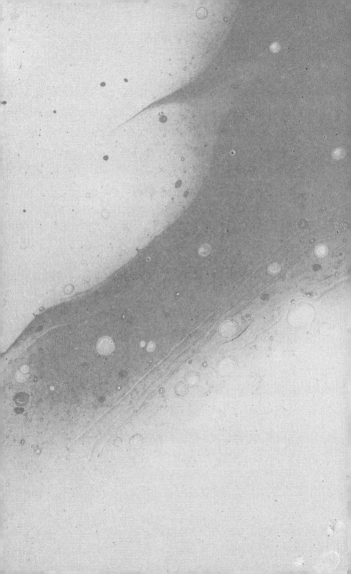

1965—around sixty years ago, almost 350 years after the first Africans were brought to North America to be slaves.[4] And that's just one issue. If it took centuries for Black people living in America to be given the right to vote, and another 95 years for that right to be protected, then we shouldn't be surprised to find evidence of racism still at work in our social systems.

Today, some hold the belief that everything about our country is racist, and others believe that racism has been completely eradicated, or at least reduced to the individual level. No one wants to be called a racist, and no one wants to believe it about themselves. But refusing to discuss a problem never makes it go away. It just makes us unprepared to deal with it when it arises in a way we can't dismiss.

WHAT DOES SCRIPTURE SAY ABOUT RACISM?

LIKE ANY KIND OF BEHAVIOR that treats one person or group of people as less than another, racism is a sin. In Genesis 1:27, we are told that "God created man in his own image, in the image of God he created him; male and female he created them." There is no hierarchy of people—there are no lesser humans in God's design. In fact, even sociologists assert that the word *race* arbitrarily sorts people into groups that don't have any biological basis.[5] All humans, regardless of appearance, are created in the image of God. Participating in racism—denying that someone is an *imago dei* creature—is definitively sinful. Beyond any politics, any moral discussion, any stereotypes or history, to treat another person as somehow less valuable because of their ethnicity is wrong in the eyes of God.

We also know that racism is not a new sin. The ancient Egyptians enslaved the

Israelites because they feared being over-powered, suggesting that there was a firm distinction between who was considered Egyptian and who was not.[6] Though historical sources differ widely regarding the skin color of Egyptians and Israelites, we know that the latter would have been considered a racial group given that they shared common biological traits, came from a certain geographic region, etc.

The New Testament sometimes describes different groups' feelings toward each other in ways that communicate the existence of racism in the culture. Samaritans, with whom, according to John 4:9, "Jews have no dealings," were not only religiously divided from Jews, but were actually an entirely different ethnic group.[7] Ancient Romans also practiced racial discrimination against the Jews. Roman historian Tacitus identified the Jews as "a race . . . prone to lust," and wrote that they "profane all that we hold sacred; on the other hand, they permit all that we abhor" and were "base and abominable."[8]

Jesus' life and ministry took place in a world that was even more racially divided than America today. Yet one core tenet of His teaching was that under God, all were equal. The Kingdom of God was open to the Gentiles as well as the Jews, an idea the Jewish religious leaders vehemently rejected. The problem of Jews rejecting Gentiles was so prevalent that Paul even affirmed in Galatians 3:28 that there was no hierarchy of any kind, no matter what earthly discrimination might exist: "There is neither Jew nor Greek, there is neither slave nor free, there is no male and female, for you are all one in Christ Jesus."

If we as Christians are to follow Jesus' example, we must accept that there is no room for racism or discrimination of any kind in our lives.

Jesus actively sought out society's out-casts and those for whom discrimination was a part of daily life. At the beginning of the book of Matthew, Jesus' genealogy—which would have traditionally only listed men—includes five women, two of whom were foreigners: Rahab (a prostitute from Jericho) and Ruth (a widow from Moab). The first time Jesus revealed Himself as the Messiah in the Gospel of John (John 4:26) was to a Samaritan woman with a checkered past.[9] With His twelve disciples, Jesus refuted the very concept of group hierarchy. For example, though Simon the Zealot and Matthew were both eth-nically Jewish, Zealots considered them-selves to be more truly Jewish than those who did not subscribe to their beliefs.[10] On the other hand, Matthew's status as a tax collector prohibited him from taking part in any Jewish religious practice, and many would have refused to call him a

Jew at all.[11] Yet both walked with Jesus as His closest friends. They were sent out during His ministry to perform miracles and preach the gospel, and were even martyred for their unwavering faithfulness to it.[12]

If we as Christians are to follow Jesus' example, we must accept that there is no room for racism or discrimination of any kind in our lives. We must show those around us the love, dignity, and respect due to humans made in the image of God, recognizing that Jesus taught, healed, forgave, and died for all of us.

WHY DOES GEN Z CARE ABOUT RACISM?

GEN Z IS THE MOST racially and ethnically diverse generation America has ever seen. Only 52 percent are white, and the Census Bureau predicts that white people will be the minority in this generation by 2026.[13] In other words, the issue of race is personal to them in a way it might not have been to previous generations. This will only become truer as Gen Zers start to get married and have children. The oldest Gen Zers turn 26 in 2023, so that stage of life is already here for some of them.[14]

According to a survey conducted by YPulse, as of January 2023 the issue of racism is second in a list of the top five social justice concerns for Gen Z.[15] And not only is the issue important to members of Gen Z, but they believe they have the power to make a difference. According to a survey by Wunderman

Thompson Data, 75 percent of Gen Zers believe that their generation will change the world for the better.[16] Racism matters to Gen Z because they don't see it as an inevitable part of life, and many of them are determined to make a positive change in our country and across the world.

Racism matters to Gen Z because they don't see it as an inevitable part of life, and many of them are determined to make a positive change in our country and across the world.

HOW DO I HAVE A CONVERSATION WITH MY TEEN ABOUT RACISM?

AS A PARENT OR CARING ADULT, you don't have to agree with everything your teen is saying about racism or how they're saying it, but approaching them openly and with questions and curiosity can create a foundation of trust and safety. Genuine interest in your teen's convictions can help remove any defensiveness they might feel.

Statistically, only 34 percent of Gen X (the generation that largely parents Gen Z) believe racial and ethnic diversity is good for the country, compared to 51 percent of Gen Z.[17] Because of the way older generations are sometimes represented on social media, members of Gen Z might be prepared to fight every time someone older starts a conversation about race. Patient, empathetic, genuine listening can help create a neutral space where your teen is more likely to unpack their beliefs with you rather than resorting to accusation and stereotypes.

Another important element of a productive conversation about race with a young person is depoliticization. As we discussed above, though race may be a huge topic in politics, politics only matter because they affect people. Describing the sin of racism as only "liberal" or "conservative" falsely assumes that this sin only exists on one side of the political aisle or the other. Anyone, regardless of their political affiliation, can hold racist beliefs, even if they don't know it. Racism isn't limited to neo-Nazis or the Ku Klux Klan. In Matthew 5:22-30, Jesus says that anger can't be justified just because you haven't murdered someone, and lust can't be justified just because you haven't committed adultery. In the same way, perpetuating racial stereotypes can't be

Being vulnerable about
the things we don't
know and about the
ways we ourselves have
failed models a posture
of being open to God's
convicting Spirit.

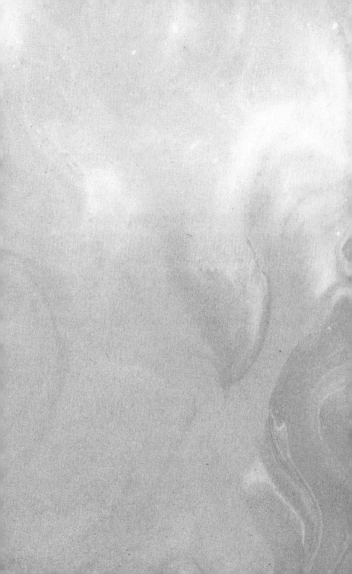

justified just because you haven't committed a hate crime.

Honesty and humility can play a huge part in conversations with our teens. Assuming that we are above reproach in every way does not create a space where our teens feel free to express themselves and their feelings—or even free to misspeak or say something incorrect without fear of backlash. Being vulnerable about the things we don't know and about the ways we ourselves have failed models a posture of being open to God's convicting Spirit.

As RaisingChildren.net.au puts it, "The stronger your relationship with your child, the more influence you'll have, because your child will be more likely to seek your guidance and value your opinion and support. In fact, if you have a strong relationship as your child becomes a young adult, they'll probably end up with values, beliefs and behaviour that are similar to yours."[18]

ALL YOU WHO ARE WEARY

IN COMPLEX, EMOTIONAL, personal, and espe-
cially political conversations with your
teen, it's essential to behave the same
way you want them to behave. If you
want your teen to start conversations
with you, trust you, respect you, and listen to your opinions and advice, you have
to do the same with them. The dynamic
will be different since you are an adult
and they are not, but that does not mean
you shouldn't treat them as a valued and
unique individual whose opinions and
beliefs are just as important as yours.

Above all, keep Christ at the center of
your conversations about race. Return
to the language Scripture uses to speak
about oppression and discrimination;
emphasize Jesus' passion for society's
mistreated people and the equality of
all believers under God. If a significant
instance of racial injustice becomes a

topic of public conversation, pray for the people involved—at mealtimes or during family devotions. Pray with your teen for the wisdom to speak with love and truth, and to articulate yourselves clearly and winsomely when you talk with each other and those around you. Pray for your teen to experience the heart of Christ for those who are suffering. And be bold to pray that God would reveal any sinful thoughts or even subconscious beliefs that don't respect others as God's image bearers.

Conversations with your teen about race will often be difficult, and they won't always go the way you want them to. But that doesn't mean they aren't worth pursuing. Racism is an issue that many teens feel strongly about, and you have the opportunity to help root them in scriptural truth. This truth will serve as

Above all, keep Christ
at the center of your
conversations about race.
Emphasize Jesus' passion
for society's mistreated
people and the equality of
all believers under God.

a foundation as they form opinions and behaviors and walk alongside their peers. With God's help, these opinions and behaviors could change the world.

RECAP

- Racism is a problem in America, but discussions of it can be controversial.

- Racism can be a matter of individual beliefs and behaviors, but it also exists at the systemic level.

- Racism is a sin according to Scripture. God made all people in His image.

- A big part of Jesus' ministry included active engagement with people who experienced racism and discrimination. In Him, there are no hierarchies.

- Racism is personal to Gen Z because they are the most diverse generation yet and they believe they can make a real impact on the world.

- It's important to have conversations with your teen about racism, both because they will encounter it and because they care about it.

- It's important to be honest about your own feelings, emotions, experiences, and even prejudices.

- Anyone can be racist, regardless of their political affiliation.

- It's essential to keep Christ at the center of conversations about racism and to ask for His grace and peace.

It's important to have conversations with your teen about racism, both because they will encounter it and because they care about it.

PERSONAL REFLECTION QUESTIONS

1. What have been your experiences with racism, either in your own life or in what you've observed and learned from others?

_____

_____

_____

_____

_____

_____

_____

_____

_____

_____

_____

_____

_____

_____

_____

2. How do you hear racism talked about in your community? What about in the media or online?

_____

_____

_____

_____

_____

_____

_____

_____

_____

_____

_____

_____

_____

_____

_____

_____

_____

_____

3. What does it look like to treat other people as fellow bearers of God's image?

_____

_____

_____

_____

_____

_____

_____

_____

_____

_____

_____

_____

_____

_____

_____

_____

_____

4. Where else does Scripture talk about how God wants us to treat foreigners and outcasts? What does it say?

_____

_____

_____

_____

_____

_____

_____

_____

_____

_____

_____

_____

_____

_____

_____

_____

_____

5. What do you think Jesus might have to say about racial issues in America?

_____

_____

_____

_____

_____

_____

_____

_____

_____

_____

_____

_____

_____

_____

_____

_____

_____

_____

6. How can you show grace to yourself
   when a conversation about race with
   your teen doesn't turn out how you
   expected it would?

_____
_____
_____
_____
_____
_____
_____
_____
_____
_____
_____
_____
_____
_____
_____
_____

7. What are things you can do to intentionally practice compassion for your teen during difficult conversations about race?

_____

_____

_____

_____

_____

_____

_____

_____

_____

_____

_____

_____

_____

_____

_____

_____

DISCUSSION QUESTIONS

1. In your own words, how would you define racism?

_____

_____

_____

_____

_____

_____

_____

_____

_____

_____

_____

_____

_____

_____

_____

2. Why do you think the topic of racism has been so controversial in recent years?

_____

_____

_____

_____

_____

_____

_____

_____

_____

_____

_____

_____

_____

_____

_____

_____

3. How do you hear people talking about racism online?

_____
_____
_____
_____
_____
_____
_____
_____
_____
_____
_____
_____
_____
_____
_____
_____
_____

4. How do you think Christians should respond to the issue of racism?

_____

_____

_____

_____

_____

_____

_____

_____

_____

_____

_____

_____

_____

_____

_____

_____

_____

_____

5. Have you ever felt like you were being discriminated against? What were the circumstances?

_____

_____

_____

_____

_____

_____

_____

_____

_____

_____

_____

_____

_____

_____

_____

_____

6. Can you think of a time you were prejudiced or biased against someone else? Why did you feel that way?

_____

_____

_____

_____

_____

_____

_____

_____

_____

_____

_____

_____

_____

_____

_____

_____

7. What are some practical ways we can show God's love to foreigners, immigrants, and refugees in our community?

_____

_____

_____

_____

_____

_____

_____

_____

_____

_____

_____

_____

_____

_____

_____

8. What can we do as a family to pursue
   racial justice?

_____

_____

_____

_____

_____

_____

_____

_____

_____

_____

_____

_____

_____

_____

_____

_____

_____

ADDITIONAL
RESOURCES

WEBSITES

- AND Campaign (andcampaign.org): a Christian organization pursuing redemptive justice through biblical values and social justice

- Equal Justice Initiative (eji.org): a nonprofit committed to ending mass incarceration and excessive punishment in the United States and protecting basic human rights for the most vulnerable people in American society

MOVIES

- *13th*, a documentary exploring the history of racial inequality in the United States

- *Just Mercy*, based on the case of Walter McMillian, a Black man sentenced to death despite evidence proving his innocence

- *Selma*, based on Martin Luther King Jr.'s crossing of the Edmund Pettus Bridge in Selma, Alabama, during the Civil Rights Movement

VIDEOS

- "Housing Segregation and Redlining in America: A Short History" (NPR)

- "Missing Chapter" (Vox): video series explaining history not covered in textbooks

BOOKS

- *Talking about Race: Gospel Hope for Hard Conversations* by Isaac Adams

- *Prophetic Lament: A Call for Justice in Troubled Times* by Soong-Chan Rah

- *The Color of Compromise: The Truth about the American Church's Complicity in Racism* by Jemar Tisby

- *Divided by Faith: Evangelical Religion and the Problem of Race in America* by Michael O. Emerson and Christian Smith

- *The New Jim Crow: Mass Incarceration in the Age of Colorblindness* by Michelle Alexander

AUDIO

- *Code Switch* (NPR): conversations about race and culture from journalists of color

- *Crooked*: album by Propaganda

- "Gangland": song by Lecrae ft. Propaganda

- "Urban Apologetics" episode from *Thirty Minutes with the Perrys* podcast

NOTES

1. Juliana Menasce Horowitz, Anna Brown, and Kiana Cox, "Race in America 2019," Pew Research Center, April 9, 2019, https://www.pewresearch.org/social-trends/2019/04/09/race-in-america-2019/.

2. "What It Meant to Be Muslim in America after 9/11," NPR, September 9, 2021, https://www.npr.org/2021/09/09/1035578745/what-it-meant-to-be-muslim-in-america-after-9-11.

3. "Voting Rights Act of 1965," History.com, January 10, 2023, https://www.history.com/topics/black-history/voting-rights-act.

4. Luci Cochran, "The 1619 Landing—Virginia's First Africans Report & FAQs," Hampton History Museum, accessed March 8, 2023, https://hampton.gov/3580/The-1619-Landing-Report-FAQs.

5. Megan Gannon, "Race Is a Social Construct, Scientists Argue," *Scientific American*, February 5, 2016, https://www.scientificamerican.com/article/race-is-a-social-construct-scientists-argue/.

6. Jacob Isaacs, "Israel's Enslavement," Chabad.org, accessed March 8, 2023, https://www.chabad.org/library/article_cdo/aid/1551/jewish/Israels-Enslavement.htm.

7. "The Genetic History of the Samaritans," 23andMe, September 5, 2008, https://blog.23andme.com/articles/samaritans-genetic-history.

8. Amy S. Kaufman, "Anti-Semitism Is Older Than You Think," The Public Medievalist, May 23, 2017, https://www.publicmedievalist.com/anti-semitism-older-think/.

9. Shawna R. B. Atteberry, "The Samaritan Woman: John 4:3-42," Christian Resource Institute, 2018, https://www.crivoice.org/WT-samaritan.html.

10. "Zealot," *Encyclopedia Britannica*, accessed March 8, 2023, https://www.britannica.com/topic/Zealot.

11. James M. Rochford, "Tax Collectors in Jesus' Day," Evidence Unseen, accessed March 8, 2023, https://www.evidenceunseen.com/theology/historical-theology/tax-collectors/.

12. "What Happened to the 12 Disciples?," Faith on Hill Church, February 11, 2020, https://www.faithonhill.com/blog/what-happened-to-the-12-disciples.

13. "On the Cusp of Adulthood and Facing an Uncertain Future: What We Know about Gen Z So Far," Pew Research Center, May 14, 2020, https://www.pewresearch.org/social-trends/2020/05/14/on-the-cusp-of-adulthood-and-facing-an-uncertain-future-what-we-know-about-gen-z-so-far-2/; "Population Projections Datasets," United States Census Bureau, December 16, 2021, https://www.census.gov/programs-surveys/popproj/data/datasets.html.

14. Clare Mulroy, "What Is Gen Z's Age Range? These Are the Years That the Generation Was Born," *USA Today*, February 8, 2023, https://www.usatoday.com/story/news/2023/02/08/gen-z-explained/11150085002/.

15. "Which Social Causes & Issues Are Gen Z and Millennials Most Passionate about in 2023?" YPulse, February 23, 2023, https://www.ypulse.com/article/2023/02/23/which-social-causes-issues-are-gen-z-and-millennials-most-passionate-about-in-2023/.

16. "New Trend Report: Generation Z: Building a Better Normal," Wunderman Thompson, December 2, 2020, https://www.wundermanthompson.com/insight/new-trend-report-generation-z-building-a-better-normal.

17. Kim Parker, Nikki Graf, and Ruth Igielnik, "Generation Z Looks a Lot like Millennials on Key Social and Political Issues," Pew Research Center, January 17, 2019, https://www.pewresearch.org/social-trends/2019/01/17/generation-z-looks-a-lot-like-millennials-on-key-social-and-political-issues/.

18. "Parents: Role Models and Positive Influences for Pre-Teens and Teenagers," RaisingChildren.net.au, May 11, 2021, https://raisingchildren.net.au/pre-teens/behaviour/encouraging-good-behaviour/being-a-role-model.

PARENT GUIDES TO SOCIAL MEDIA
BY AXIS

It's common to feel lost in your teen's world. Let these be your go-to guides on social media, how it affects your teen, and how to begin an ongoing conversation about faith that matters.

BUNDLE THESE 5 BOOKS AND SAVE

www.axis.org

CP1805

PARENT GUIDES TO FINDING TRUE IDENTITY
BY AXIS

When culture is constantly pulling teens away from Christian values, let these five parent guides spark an ongoing conversation about finding your true identity in Christ.

BUNDLE THESE 5 BOOKS AND SAVE

PARENT GUIDES TO CONNECTING IN CHAOS
BY AXIS

When grief, death, racism, or cancel culture rock your teen's world, it can be tough to connect. These concise guides offer deep insights and clear strategies to approach these triggering topics with confidence.

BUNDLE THESE 5 BOOKS AND SAVE

www.axis.org

CP1915